Spitfire

THE

INSIDE

STORY

First published in 2014

A catalogue record for this book is available from the British Library

ISBN: 978-0-85733-716-0

Published by Haynes Publishing, Sparkford, Yeovil,
Somerset BA22 7JJ, UK
Tel: 01963 442030 Fax: 01963 440001
Int. tel: +44 1963 442030 Int. fax: +44 1963 440001
E-mail: sales@haynes.co.uk
Website: www.haynes.co.uk

Haynes North America Inc., 861 Lawrence Drive, Newbury Park, California 91320, USA

Images © Mirrorpix

Creative Director: Kevin Gardner
Designed for Haynes by BrainWave

Printed and bound in the US

Spitfire

THE
INSIDE
STORY

David Curnock

Contents

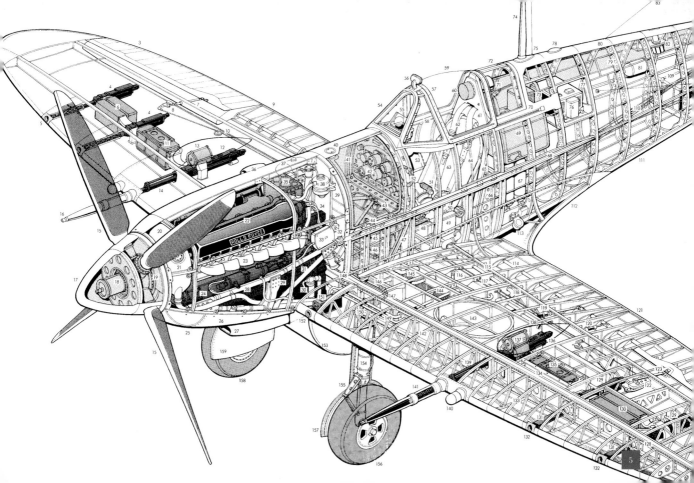

ROLLS ROYCE

5

"The 'Spitfire' is a single-seat day and night fighter monoplane built to the Air Ministry specification. It is a low-wing cantilever monoplane with the inner sections sloping down to the undercarriage enclosures. It has a Rolls-Royce 'Goshawk' steam-cooled engine with condensers built into the wing surfaces. Armament consists of four machine-guns."

– Supermarine announcing the Spitfire in 1934

◗ This Mark PRXI Spitfire, flown by Martin Sargeant, is pictured against the backdrop of the Kent cliffs in 2000. This aircraft was later destroyed in an accident at Rouen Airfield, Normandy, during an air show in June 2001.

Introducing Britain's Greatest Ever Fighter

Designed by R J Mitchell, the Supermarine Spitfire is known throughout the world for the historic part it played in the defence of Britain during the Second World War. It evolved from a purely interceptor fighter into a versatile, all-round asset. Serving in every operational theatre in a variety of roles, it was, variously, a fighter, fighter-bomber, fighter-reconnaissance, and long-range, photo-reconnaissance aircraft, while naval versions also served from the decks of aircraft carriers. Making its maiden flight on 5th March 1936, the Spitfire remained in front-line service in the Royal Air Force until 1954.

By the end of its development cycle, the Spitfire had a power output that was double that of the first production aircraft. Its maximum take-off weight and rate of climb had both doubled, maximum speed was a third greater than the original, and its firepower was an almost unbelievable fivefold increase over the first operational version. During the years of development, subtle changes to the airframe were made, including modifications to the profile and area of the fin and rudder, while its elegant wing shape was, on some marks, either clipped or extended, to fulfil a specific role.

◗ A replica of the Spitfire prototype pictured at Duxford on 2nd May 1998. The original prototype was destroyed in a landing accident on 4th September 1939, the day following the declaration of war against Germany.

Mitchell's brilliant and distinctive wing design proved as adaptable as the rest of the Spitfire's airframe. Various configurations provided a range of armaments and reconnaissance cameras, while some featured an increased internal fuel capacity. The Spitfire was the only British military aircraft to remain in full-scale production throughout the Second World War and was produced in greater numbers than any other British combat aircraft. In production for more than 12 years, a total of 20,351 Spitfires were built in 22 variants. This figure does not include Seafires (originally known as Sea Spitfires), of which 2,334 were produced for the Royal Navy. Early Spitfires were sometimes "recycled" to form the basis of later marks.

Rightfully recognized as having played a major role not only in the defence of Britain but also in the ultimate Allied victory in the Second World War, the iconic Spitfire is considered by many to have been the most successful piston-engined fighter of all time, justifiably deserving both its place in British history, and the accolade of being one of the all-time greats in the world of military aviation.

◆ An article in the *Daily Mirror* on 19th June 1936, read as follows:

NEW ONE-MAN FIGHTER

Believed to be capable of about 300 m.p.h., the Vickers Supermarine Spitfire, fastest military plane in the world, demonstrated at Southampton yesterday. It is a single seater, day and night fighter, beautifully streamlined and equipped, with a twelve-cylinder V-shaped liquid-cooled Rolls-Royce Merlin engine, developing higher horse-power than any other at present in use in the R.A.F. It is the same engine as in the Fairey Battle bomber. Nothing was given out concerning yesterday's speed and general performance. The machine's design owes much to the work of the Supermarine Aviation Works, which built the Schneider Trophy victor.

THE DAILY MIRROR, Friday, June 19, 1936.

Daily Mirror
THE DAILY PICTURE NEWSPAPER WITH THE LARGEST NET SALE

Broadcasting—Pages 22 & 23

WEEK'S WEATHER CHART —Page 10

No. 10,156   Registered at the G.P.O. as a Newspaper.   FRIDAY, JUNE 19, 1936   One Penny

Amusements: Pages 24 and 25

QUADS TO BE ON SHOW—6D. A LOOK

Only Way to Balance Budget

PUBLIC FUND FAILS

FROM OUR SPECIAL CORRESPONDENT.

Britain's famous quads—Ann, Paul, Ernest and Michael Miles—are going to start earning their own living when they are eight months old—in three weeks.

THEY are to be put on public exhibition in the new sun nursery that is being built on to the country home, The Oaklea, the new home of their parents.

By paying 6d. visitors will be able to walk up a staircase on to a balcony surrounding the nursery and look through windows into the room where the quads will lie in their cots.

This course has been decided upon as the only possible way of raising the money.

So far, the bulk of the cost has been borne by Dr. Harrison, who brought them into the world and who has been paying their upkeep since.

Already Cost £2,000

The only way left of meeting the steadily rising bills for their upkeep, Dr. Harrison decided, is to carry out the Canadian Quins' idea and the quads on exhibition.

Their parents have no option but to agree. Dr. Harrison's nursing home will be ready in a fortnight.

A Day with Shirley

WHAT is Shirley Temple really like? This question is answered by Reginald Whitley, the "Daily Mirror" film expert, who has just returned from Hollywood.

Two pages of photographs which tell you what to spend and what he says about a day he spent with the charming, supremedom little girl who, at seven years of age, is the sweetheart of the world.

GIRL PAT IS "SIGHTED" AGAIN

Mystery Deepens

MYSTERY OF THE GIRL PAT, THE TRUANT GRIMSBY TRAWLER, DEEPENED LAST NIGHT.

Milady in a Fix

Victorian crinolines and modern car set a problem for little bridesmaid found for the wedding at Christ Church, Shldesley, Manchester, yesterday of Captaine B. Whipp and Miss Noreen Oarlton.

The King George—Sister Ship for the Queen Mary

RIFLE AND GAS "WAR" ROUND U.S. FACTORY

FROM OUR OWN CORRESPONDENT.

"DEAD SOLDIERS" IN CARNIVAL

LIFE AMBITION TO KILL A GIRL

Friday, June 19, 1936   THE DAILY MIRROR   London Edition   Page 3

SANCTIONS PERIL IS AIR WAR IN A DAY

"No More Until We Are Stronger"
—MR. BALDWIN

FASTEST EVER BUILT

WITH sanctions at last dead, Mr. Stanley Baldwin stood up in the House of Commons last night, announced his line, told the country just why sanctions were "midsummer madness" in these words:—

NEW ONE-MAN FIGHTER

Referred to in capable of about 300 m.p.h., the Vickers supermarine Spitfire, fastest military 'plane in the world, demonstrated at Southampton yesterday.

Socialist Censure Vote

"The Cowards"

20,000 Sign Petition

HEBRIDES AND BACK 36 HOURS

TRAIN ON HAGGIS—FREE

FREED EIGHT YEARS AFTER DEATH SENTENCE

"In the Army," Thought His Son

WITH tears of joy in his eyes, eight-year-old Jimmy Dolson, of Chester, to-day excitedly greeted his father, who had never seen his family since Jimmy was a baby a few months old.

DAWN WATCH FOR THE SHADOW ON THE SUN

Six Years of Dyspepsia

WOMAN WHO WAS AFRAID TO EAT

FEWER KILLED, MORE INJURED

11

"The Spitfire was immensely strong: a pilot had no need to fear the danger of pulling the wings off, no matter how desperate the situation became."

– Douglas Bader

◗ A contemporary photograph of a Griffon-powered Spitfire in flight, c.1941. Note the modified shape of the nose profile which follows closely around the outline of the engine camshaft covers.

The Spitfire – Design and Development

Reginald Joseph (R J) Mitchell, joined the Supermarine (later, Vickers-Supermarine) company in 1917. His brilliance was soon recognized and he was appointed Chief Designer only two years later. Primarily involved in the design of fighters, bombers and flying boats, he first came to public attention with his excellent series of racing aircraft that took part in the Schneider Trophy races, winning the trophy outright after three victories, with his Supermarine S6B. However, his name will eternally be linked with his greatest ever brainchild, the Spitfire. The unmistakeable elliptical shape of the Spitfire's wing plan form resulted from the work of Beverley Shenstone, Mitchell's chief aerodynamics engineer whose work was admired by experts and laymen alike.

Following Mitchell's death in 1937, the onus for developing the Spitfire project fell onto the shoulders of the designer's chief draughtsman, Joseph "Joe" Smith, who was appointed to succeed him. Often termed "the forgotten designer", Smith oversaw the project that kept the Spitfire at the forefront of Britain's air defences throughout the war and beyond. Although his name is not well known to the public at large, the work of Smith and his team kept the Spitfire abreast of developments in enemy fighters.

▶ The Supermarine S6B won the Schneider Trophy outright for Britain in 1931. Its designer, R J Mitchell, pictured second from right, was responsible for the design of the iconic Spitfire fighter aircraft of the Second World War.

Perhaps Smith's greatest contribution was the work involved in the introduction of the Griffon-engined series of Spitfires, which increased their speed and altitude capabilities beyond the limits of the Merlin-engined versions. With this more powerful engine came new challenges: to counter the increased torque and power output of the Griffon, the team redesigned the tail unit, strengthened the wings and modified the undercarriage. Innovations such as a pressurized cockpit, camera installations and changes in armaments were also introduced under the guidance of Smith. His contribution to the story of the Spitfire was immense, a fact later recognized in the award of a CBE.

▶ Spitfire LF Mark XII, MB878, was built between July 1943 and March 1944. Powered by a Rolls-Royce Griffon IV engine, it was used at the Aeroplane and Armament Experimental Establishment at Boscombe Down, Wiltshire, during September 1943, for trials with a 500lb bomb on its centre-fuselage rack.

"'She really was a perfect flying machine,' said one pilot. I often marvelled at how this plane could be so easy and civilized to fly and yet how it could be such an effective fighter."

– A Californian who flew with the Royal Air Force in the Battle of Britain

◗ The evocative sight of a Spitfire PR Mark XI alongside the famous White Cliffs of Dover during celebrations marking the 60th Anniversary of the Battle of Britain, September 2000.

The Spitfire – Marks and Variants

Although many people admired and respected the brilliance of Mitchell's 300-series Spitfire, few could have imagined the breadth of its development that took place under his successor, Joe Smith. From the original prototype, there were to follow a total of 24 separate marks and many sub-variants. Although the classic, Rolls-Royce Merlin-engined Spitfires took much of the glory in the Battle of Britain, the advent of the same maker's larger and more powerful Griffon engine provided the means with which Smith and his team could develop the Spitfire such that it remained in front-line service throughout the war.

It was Smith's desire to install the Griffon in the Spitfire as early as 1940 but the wartime situation dictated that all efforts should be concentrated on the Merlin-engined variants. The first flight of a Griffon-engined Spitfire eventually took place in November 1941. Coupled with Mitchell's adaptable wing design, which enabled a variety of armament options, the new engine provided the power that helped this iconic aircraft prove its versatility in many roles and in every theatre of operations. The following section gives brief details of the significant differences between the various marks that existed within the Spitfire family tree.

◗ Spitfires on the production line at Castle Bromwich Aircraft Factory in 1944.

Supermarine Type 224 – Built to Air Ministry Specification F7/30, the first ever Spitfire was a gull-winged monoplane with a fixed landing gear in "trouser" fairings; it had a 600hp Rolls-Royce Goshawk engine and four machine-guns. Performance was disappointing, and the Type 224 was relegated to become a target on a firing range at Orford Ness, Suffolk, in summer 1937.

Supermarine Type 300 – Spitfire Prototype: K5054 was first flown in March 1936. Powered by a Rolls-Royce Merlin engine, the Spitfire prototype had a top speed of 342mph, exceeding all expectations.

Type 300 – Spitfire Mark IA and IB: The first production version of the Spitfire, with either a Merlin II or III engine, it had a top speed of 364mph. The Mark IA was armed with eight 0.303 Browning machine-guns, while the Mark IB had four 0.303 Browning machine-guns and two 20mm Hispano cannon. They entered service in 1938 with Nos 19 and 66 Squadrons. 1,566 were produced.

◀ Spitfire I (K9942) in the colour scheme and code letters of No. 72 Squadron, on display at the RAF Museum, Cosford, 2011.

Type 329 – Spitfire Mark II: Similar to the Mark I, except for the engine – a 1,175hp Merlin XII. It had a top speed of 370mph, and 920 were built.

Types 330 and 348 – Spitfire Mark III: Only two Mark IIIs were produced. With a 1,390hp Merlin XX, this was the first Spitfire to have a constant-speed propeller, a retractable tailwheel and clipped wing-tips. Its top speed was around 385mph.

Type 337 – Spitfire PR Mark IV: The first unarmed reconnaissance version. With an integral fuel tank in each wing leading edge, a long-range fuel tank behind the pilot, and an additional oil tank in the port wing gun bay, this mark had a range of up to 2,000 miles. It was fitted with two downward-facing cameras and, sometimes, an oblique camera in the rear fuselage.

◀ A staged photograph of Spitfire pilots during a "scramble" during the Battle of Britain, 1940.

Type 349 – Spitfire Mark V: This mark was the mainstay of Britain's fighter strength for much of the war and served in many theatres of operation. 6,479 were built. Some Mark Vs had clipped wing-tips to improve their rate of roll. It was produced in three versions:

(1) Mark VA – armed with eight 0.303 Browning machine-guns.

(2) Mark VB – four 0.303 Browning machine-guns and two 20mm Hispano cannon.

(3) Mark VC – four 20mm cannon or a combination of cannon and machine-guns.

Type 350 – Spitfire Mark VI: Only 100 were produced. The Mark VI was optimized for high-altitude interception, with a Merlin 47 engine driving a four-bladed propeller, extended wing-tips for improved performance at high altitudes and a partially pressurized cockpit.

◀ Spitfires of the Bombay Squadron during a section scramble in November 1943.

Types 351 and 360 – Spitfire Mark VII: Powered by a Merlin 60- or 70-series engine, with larger, symmetrical under-wing radiators, extended wing-tips, a larger rudder and a pressurized cockpit. Its top speed was 416mph.

Type 359 – Spitfire Mark VIII: An unpressurized version of the Mark VII. It had standard, clipped, or extended wing-tips, according to operational requirements.

Type 361 – Spitfire Mark IX: This was the second most numerous mark – 5,665 were built. Early examples from 1942 were converted from strengthened Mark V airframes. With a Merlin 61- or 63-series engine, it was capable of 409mph at 28,000ft. Its service ceiling was an astounding 43,000ft. With a Merlin 66 engine, this mark was designated LF Mark IX and optimized for low- and medium-altitude combat. High-altitude versions, with the Merlin 70, were designated HF Mark IX. Most Mark IXs were built with the C-wing. From 1944, some were built with the E-wing.

◗ A Spitfire LF Mark IX makes a low pass along the runway at RAF St Athan, November 1997.

Types 387, 365 and 370 – Spitfire PR Mark X and PR Mark XI: Just 16 PR Mark X Spitfires (Type 387) were built. These were basically PR Mark VIIs but renumbered due to a policy change. The PR Mark X was based on the Mark VII airframe, with wings and camera layout from the PR Mark XI, and had a pressurized cockpit.

Type 365 (standard) and Type 370 (tropical) – Spitfire PR Mark XI: This was a hybrid derived from the Marks VII, VIII and IX, and was the first PR variant to carry two vertical F52, 36in focal length cameras in the rear fuselage. It is visually identifiable by its wraparound windscreen, deeper nose (housing a larger oil tank), and retractable tailwheel.

Type 366 – Spitfire Mark XII: This interim mark was the first to be fitted with the new Rolls-Royce Griffon engine. Most examples had a new wing structure with clipped wing-tips, retractable tailwheels, and were optimized for low-altitude interception duties.

Type 367 – Spitfire Mark XIII: Fitted with a new, specially rated, low-level Merlin 32 engine, 26 were converted from early PR versions or Mark Vs. They were first used for low-level reconnaissance for the Normandy landings.

◀ A worm's eye view of a Spitfire XII from No. 41 Squadron, taken in April 1944.

Type 379 – Spitfire Mark XIV: Powered by the 2,050hp Griffon 65 with a five-bladed propeller, this variant was based on the Mark VIII airframe; some had the "cut-down" rear fuselage and bubble canopy, and deeper radiator housings. The longer Griffon engine altered the contour of the Mark XIV's fuselage forward of the cockpit. This mark proved the most successful Spitfire against the V-1 flying bombs. Some high-back Mark XIVs were converted to become fighter-reconnaissance FR Mark XIVs with a single camera facing either to port or starboard. 957 Mark XIVs were built, of which 430 were FR Mark XIVs.

Mark XV and Mark XVII – These were mark numbers reserved for the naval version, the Seafire, to coordinate the numbering systems (no type numbers were allocated).

♦ This Spitfire XIVC, serial number RM689, pictured here in 1990, was involved in an accident at Woodford Air Show in 1992, in which the pilot, David Moore, lost his life. Owned by Rolls-Royce, the wreckage was placed in storage with the intention of rebuilding it to flying condition.

Type 361 – Spitfire Mark XVI: Basically a Mark IX fitted with the US-built, low-altitude Packard Merlin 266. All had clipped wings and additional rear fuselage fuel tanks; many featured the low-deck rear fuselage and bubble canopy. Armament was two 20mm Hispano cannon and two 0.50in heavy machine-guns, one 500lb bomb under the fuselage, and a 250lb bomb under each wing. 1,054 were produced.

Type 394 – Spitfire Mark XVIII: Sometimes referred to as the Mark 18 (Arabic numerals), this was a refinement of the Mark XIV and appeared in both fighter and fighter-reconnaissance versions. Too late for war service, this mark was used against guerrilla forces in the Malayan Emergency.

Types 389 and 390 – Spitfire Mark XIX: Based on the PR Mark XI, it was powered by the Griffon 65-series engine. Later versions (Type 390) had a pressurized cockpit and a fuel capacity triple that of the original Mark I Spitfire. In front-line RAF service until 1954, a total of 225 were built.

▶ A photo-reconnaissance Spitfire Mark XIX. These unarmed aircraft flew long-range missions over enemy territory to bring back intelligence pictures of strategic targets from as far afield as Berlin and Stettin, on the Baltic coast.

Type 366 – Spitfire Mark XX: This designation was given to the two Mark IV Griffon-engined prototypes.

Type 356 – Spitfire Mark 21: The first mark number to be officially designated in Arabic numerals. Essentially a Mark XIV airframe with redesigned and strengthened wings, larger ailerons, and a new, longer undercarriage to provide ground clearance for the larger, five-bladed propeller of its Griffon 61 engine. The longer undercarriage legs incorporated a set of links to shorten the legs when retracting, to allow them to fit into the original-sized wheel wells. The Mark 21 saw little action at the end of the war and only 120 were built.

Type 356 – Spitfire Mark 22: Almost identical to the Mark 21 (hence the same maker's type number), except for the low-deck rear fuselage, bubble canopy, larger tail surfaces, and a 24-volt electrical system instead of the 12-volt system of previous marks. 287 were built.

Type 372 – Spitfire Mark 23: This type was never built. A modified wing with an increased angle of incidence, was intended to be fitted to a Mark 22, thus becoming a Mark 23. When flown in tests while fitted to a Mark VIII, this proved unsatisfactory and the concept was abandoned.

◀ Spitfire Mark F22s from RAF Ouston, pictured during the 1949 Battle of Britain celebrations near to their home base.

Prominent in this skeleton drawing of a Spitfire are the two
cannon and four machine-guns in the wings. A blister fairing on
each wing's upper surface covers the ammunition feed drum for
each cannon.

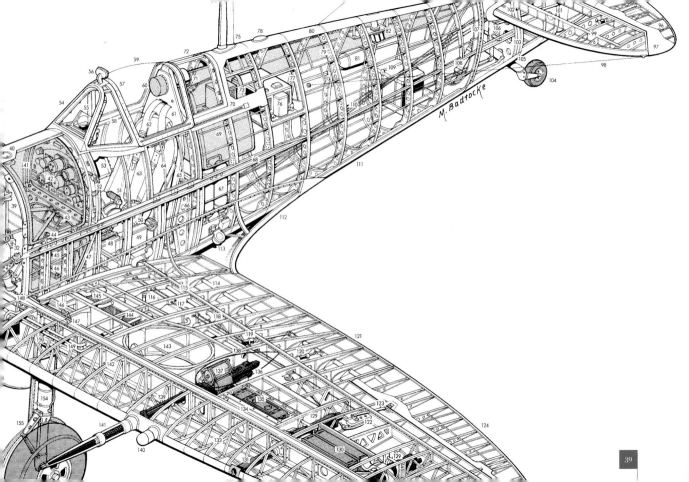

M. Badtocke

39

Type 356 – Spitfire Mark 24: The final version of the Spitfire, of which 81 were built. It was similar to the Mark 22 but with increased fuel capacity, rocket projectile rails under the wings, four 20mm Hispano cannon, and bomb racks under the fuselage and wings. The Mark 24 was twice as heavy, more than twice as powerful, and showed an increase in climb rate of 80 per cent over that of the prototype.

Type 509 – Spitfire Trainer TR Mark IX (Tr 9): After the war, around 30 Spitfire Mark IXs were bought by Vickers-Armstrong: 21 were converted to become the Trainer (Tr) Mark IX. The front cockpit was moved 13 inches forwards and a second cockpit (with dual controls, raised seat and high-domed canopy) was added behind it. Several were purchased by the Irish Air Corps.

Types 355 and 359 – Spitfire Float Planes: The German invasion of Norway in 1940 prompted the conversion of an existing Spitfire into an experimental float plane version. A Mark I, R6722, nicknamed "Narvik Nightmare" was modified with the addition of floats from a Blackburn Roc, however, the urgent need for Spitfires at home caused this aircraft to be converted back to its land-based status without being flown.

◀ A Spitfire F Mark 24, photographed while serving with the Royal Hong Kong Auxiliary Air Force in 1949. This beautiful aircraft can be seen on display at the Imperial War Museum, Duxford.

Type 323 – Speed Spitfire: In an attempt to gain the world speed record, the 48th Mark I off the production line, K9834, was modified with the installation of a new Merlin II engine and a four-bladed propeller that produced one-third more power than its predecessor. All military equipment was deleted, the aircraft's skin was smoothed with flush riveting, access panel gaps were filled, the tailwheel was replaced by a skid, and the windscreen and canopy were streamlined.

A rare two-seat version of the Spitfire. TE 308 started life as a Mark IX but in 1950 she was converted to a two-seater trainer. Designated the Type 509, sometimes known as the Mark TR9, TE 308 was one of six delivered to the Irish Air Corps. Later sold to an American owner, this unusual version of the Spitfire has been a regular attraction at air shows in the USA. It wears the fictional code letters RJ-M in memory of the Spitfire's designer R J Mitchell.

A Spitfire Mark XIV bearing the squadron code letters of No. 350 (Belgian) Squadron, c. 1990. This fine aircraft is currently undergoing a complete rebuild following a fatal crash at an air display in 1992.

This PR Mark XIX painted with D-Day invasion stripes shows off its elegant lines in a topside pass at an air show.

"The Seafire had such delightful upright flying qualities that knowing it had an inverted fuel and oil system, I decided to try inverted 'figure-8s'. They were as easy as pie, even when hanging by the complicated, but comfortable, British pilot restraint harness. I was surprised to hear myself laughing as if I were crazy. I have never enjoyed a flight in attitude. It was clear to see how few exhausted, hastily trained, Battle of Britain pilots were able to fight off Hitler's hordes for so long, and so successfully, with it."

– United States Navy pilot Corky Meyer about the Seafire fighter he test flew during the Joint USAAF/US Navy Fighter Conference in Florida, United States in March 1943

Seafires and Seafangs

During 1941 and 1942, the Admiralty carried out a programme to assess the suitability of the Spitfire as a potential fleet defence fighter to operate from the decks of Royal Navy aircraft carriers. Earlier overtures to acquire Spitfires had been rejected due to the urgent need for RAF use of the aircraft during the Battle of Britain.

In late 1941, a contract was placed for the conversion of 48 Spitfire Mark VBs to naval requirements. Modifications included strengthening of the rear fuselage and installation of an A-frame arrestor hook, resulting in the Sea Spitfire (later truncated to Seafire) Mark IB. This variant was used to gain experience of operating the type from aircraft carriers, however, the rear fuselage proved not sufficiently strong for carrier operations. A further 118 Spitfire VBs were converted, with additional strengthening around the rear fuselage access hatches; naval radio equipment was installed, and flight instrumentation was recalibrated to display nautical speed and distance measurements. Armament remained as for that on the RAF's Mark VB.

A Seafire F17 belonging to the Fleet Air Arm Museum. Note the downward-folding wing tips that were needed for below-deck headroom clearance.

The Seafire was a compromise to fill the void in the fleet defence and naval support roles. Prone to flight deck incidents, it went through many iterations before the end of a production run of 2,334 examples. Progressing through a series of modified land-based marks and naval-purpose redesigns, the Seafire was built in a number of configurations, some with folding wings, some without; others were produced with Griffon engines and different hook arrangements; some later versions (from 1943) had provision for Rocket Assisted Take-Off Gear (RATOG) to help reduce their take-off distance. Logical development of the Seafire resulted in the ultimate variant of the type that was such a drastic variation from the original that it warranted a change of name; thus was born the Seafang. With laminar-flow wings bearing little resemblance to the elliptical-shaped wings of its Seafire forebears, and an aggressive stance on a wider-track undercarriage, the perceived role of the Seafang was overtaken by the advent of the jet age: only 11 of the 18 built were flown. Like its land-based sister, the Spiteful, this aircraft was relegated to the role of research into transonic flight.

⬥ The lack of gun ports in the wing leading edges indicate that this is a photo-reconnaissance variant of the Spitfire. These aircraft provided detailed images of targets, both before and after a raid, that allowed an accurate assessment of the effectiveness of an attack on enemy installations to be made.

"The gratitude of every home in our Island, in our Empire, and indeed throughout the world, except in the abodes of the guilty, goes out to the British airmen who, undaunted by odds, unwearied in their constant challenge and mortal danger, are turning the tide of the World War by their prowess and by their devotion. Never in the field of human conflict was so much owed by so many to so few. All hearts go out to the fighter pilots, whose brilliant actions we see with our own eyes day after day."

— Winston Churchill, 20th August 1940

◗ A Spitfire and a Hurricane from the Battle of Britain Memorial Flight.

Spitfires in Action

The Spitfire, together with the Hurricane, will forever be associated with the Battle of Britain in 1940. Its story continued throughout the Second World War, making its mark in a variety of roles and in many campaigns, including the Battle of France, the Defence of Malta, the North African Campaign and in the Far East. Although the Spitfire had operated over Europe from their bases in Britain, its first overseas deployment was to the island of Malta. In 1942, Spitfires were carried on board the aircraft carriers HMS *Eagle* and the USS *Wasp*, from where they were flown to land bases on the besieged island.

Taking part in many heroic actions, the success of the Spitfire was a major factor in the outcome of the war. Behind the scenes, men and women played their part in Spitfire production, delivery and maintenance. On the squadrons, ground crews and support staff worked tirelessly to keep "their" aircraft in the air. Pilots put their lives on the line on a daily basis, with many being killed, injured or taken prisoner as a result of being shot down, as they flew their Spitfires in action against the might of the Axis onslaught.

▶ A work-stained Spitfire V, c. 1944. The clipped wing-tips are shown to good advantage in this shot, which was taken over southern England.

Mark XII Spitfires from No. 41 Squadron on patrol.

THE DAILY MIRROR, Friday, Jan. 12, 1940.

Daily Mirror

JAN. 12

No. 11,302.

ONE PENNY

Registered at the G.P.O. as a Newspaper.

THE SPIT IN THE SPITFIRE

These machine-gun feeding rounds of ammunition into a Spitfire at a Fighter Station "somewhere in England." There are eight machine-guns in the plane. Each gun fires 900 rounds a minute. It would take about fifteen seconds to fire the cartridges used in this picture. Death by the yard, you'll see!

6 AIR RAIDS ON BRITAIN

GERMAN BOMBERS, ATTACKING AT SIX POINTS ON BRITAIN YESTERDAY, MADE THE BIGGEST AIR RAID ON BRITAIN SINCE THE WAR BEGAN. THEY APPEARED OVER THE SOUTH-EAST COAST, THE THAMES ESTUARY, EAST ANGLIA, THE HUMBER, THE TYNE AND THE FIRTH OF FORTH.

No bombs fell on land. Three merchant ships off the Norfolk coast escaped when bombs fell all round them. Bombs aimed at Aberdeen trawlers missed their mark, although the planes flew so low that they seemed to skim the trawlers' masts.

One of the raiders, its petrol tank hit by bullets, was forced down in Denmark at 9.30 last night, twenty miles from the German frontier. Its crew of four burned the machine and surrendered to the police.

A.R.P. FLYING SQUAD PLAN

PEER'S SON SHOT

VICAR DUG THE GRAVE

ARCTIC GIRLS IN MEN'S PANTS

"MAN" OF THE FAMILY

"Replacement of Sunk Ships Not Nearly Fast Enough Yet"

The perfect emergency ration

Fry's Sandwich Chocolate

DAILY MIRROR, Thursday, July 11, 1940.

Daily Mirror

JULY 11

No. 11,456.

ONE PENNY

Registered at the G.P.O. as a Newspaper.

Traitors To Be Hanged

Death by hanging will be the fate of anyone found guilty of helping the enemy.

R.A.F.'s BATTLE SCORE—37

THE biggest enemy air challenge over our coasts was fought off by the R.A.F. In furious combats our fighters shot down fourteen German machines and in seriously damaged twenty - three others that they were unlikely to reach home, the Air Ministry announced early this morning. Two British machines were lost, but the pilot of one is safe.

CIVILIANS MAY BE TRIED BY ARMY

CIVILIANS, as well as men of the Services, who impede the efficient prosecution of the war, will be tried by courts-martial if a Bill read a first time in the House of Commons yesterday becomes law.

Nazi Storm Trooper in B.B.C.

FIRST AID MEN MAY NOT LEAVE

B.U.F. IS BANNED

GERMAN RADIO WAR ON FRANCE

NAZI RADIO FADES OUT

Good when you're TIRED

You've had something more than a drink when you've had a GUINNESS

Left Newspaper

Daily Mirror

MIRROR, Monday, August 12, 1940.
No. 11,443. ONE PENNY
Registered at the G.P.O. as a Newspaper.

AUG. 12

60 FALL TO R.A.F. AND GUNS

Last of a Raider

THE German Air Force launched 400 machines on a 300-mile front in attacks on our coasts and shipping yesterday—and lost at least sixty of them.

Announcing this total—which equalled last Thursday's "bag"—the Air Ministry said at midnight that the figure was based on reports received up to 9 p.m. Five of the sixty enemy machines fell to anti-aircraft guns.

The enemy attacks ranged from Portland, Dorset, to points off the East Anglian coast, where a convoy was raided.

Twenty-six British fighters were lost, but two of the pilots are safe.

Warmouth was raided. More than 200 bombers and fighters were flung against Portland—of which 150 reached the coast. And between fifty and sixty machines were over Dover.

It was over Portland and the convoy that the big air battles of the day were waged.

One hundred machines shot down, in an all-out battle. Thirty Messerschmitts, Junker Junkers.

D.F.C.'s Squadron Gets 10

Leader of the squadron already, has the D.F.C. and bar. Fighting with him yesterday was a matured officer who is nearly forty, and who shot down one of his twenty machines yesterday.

The first battle began at 7.30 a.m. over Dover. German fighters swept down to machine-gun barrage balloons, apparently to clear the way for other raiders.

The plan was a costly failure. British anti-aircraft gunners let loose a barrage of fire which shot down three Messerschmitts.

As the guns knocked out groups of raiders, a Spitfire squadron went into action above the clouds. This squadron bought four raiders during the day.

Just after 10 a.m. came the big attack on Portland. Two squadrons were slightly damaged by raiders and have building, battling a hospital ship.

Attack Which Cost Them 40

But this attack cost the Germans forty machines. Spitfires and Hurricanes squadrons roared in and out, breaking up the enemy formations, routing and diving and picking off machines in a long series of dog fights.

One of our balloons came down near a coast town.

TROOPSHIP HIT: 740 SAFE

WHEN the British transport Mohamed Ali El-Kebir (7,527 tons) was torpedoed and sunk by a U-boat in a night attack in the Atlantic, 740 survivors were handed out of a total of 860 troops and naval ratings on board.

This was announced by the Admiralty last night.

The survivors were rescued by another ship and landed at a Scottish port.

The transport liner sank in about two hours...

GHOST IN GOLOSHES IS LAID BY B.B.C.

WITH proper ceremonial the B.B.C. told the Ghost in Goloshes last night, real never again, in the house programmes at least, will his soft cammered footsteps be heard in the empty building.

TROOPSHIP HIT: 740 SAFE (photo caption)

Cabinet's Thanks to the R.A.F.

The Prime Minister has sent the following message to the Secretary for Air:—

"The Cabinet wished to send if one would convey to the fighter squadrons of the R.A.F. (displayed in Thursday's brilliant action) their admiration of the skill and prowess which they displayed, and congratulate them on the destruction of so many enemy aircraft."

89 BRITISH DOWN—NAZIS

NEW PROTECTED AREAS

The Home Secretary has made a further Aliens (Protected Areas) Order, naming the counties of Cornwall and Devon and south of Somerset as protected areas.

The Order also extends protected areas in Hants and Wiltshire and comes into effect from Thursday next.

Right Newspaper

Daily Mirror

DAILY MIRROR, Saturday, Sept. 28, 1940.
No. 11,484. ONE PENNY
Registered at the G.P.O. as a Newspaper.

SEPT. 28

FLYER V.C. AT EIGHTEEN

V.C. hero at eighteen is Sergeant John Hannah, of Glasgow, who put out a fire caused by a direct hit on the bomb rack of his machine and made it possible for the pilot to land safely.

He is the youngest V.C. of the war.

The award was announced yesterday. On the night of September 15, 1940, Hannah was the wireless operator-air gunner in an aircraft engaged in a successful attack on enemy barge concentrations at Antwerp.

It was then subjected to intense anti-aircraft fire and received a direct hit from a projectile of an explosive and incendiary nature ; both apparatus bursts inside the fuselage caused fire.

U.S. Doomed If—

Send All Quickly

PACT MAY SWAY U.S.

AS soon as President Roosevelt learned yesterday of the pact between Japan and the Axis he called his defence chiefs, State officials and Lord Lothian, Britain Ambassador for special conferences.

DICTATOR FOR HOMELESS

DICTATOR appointed to care for the air-raid homeless in London is Mr Henry Wilkins, K.C.

NEW SHELTER POWERS

Wide powers have been given to local authorities, under new defence regulations to compel use of shelters...

Hit Back, Arms Workers

To the workers in the arms factories, Mr. Herbert Morrison, Minister of Supply, issues this "Order of the Day":—

You are front line fighters in the battle for freedom. While the Nazi barbarians rain down their bombs on our people, none is the actual task of counter attack.

130 DOWN IN DAY WAR

ONE hundred and thirty raiders shot down. That was last night's official estimate of Germany's air losses yesterday.

Fierce battles raged as R.A.F. fighters ambushed mass formations of daylight raiders over the London area and many parts of South England.

Thirty-four of our fighters were missing last night but the pilots of fifteen are safe.

4-Engine Plane Down

A fight which ended with the destruction of one of Germany's latest four-engined aircraft was seen by many people at East Grinstead last night.

IF IT'S CHOCOLATE
THEN IT'S FOOD

CADBURY'S
BOURNVILLE
PLAIN FLAVOUR
CHOCOLATE
for quick energy

Eric S Lock DSO, DFC and Bar, pictured in the cockpit of his Spitfire of No. 611 (West Lancashire) Squadron. On its side are recorded his 26 kills, which he achieved in only 26 weeks of operational flying, along with his "two-fingered salute" emblem. His middle name was Stanley, although his fellow pilots nicknamed him "Sawn-off", owing to his short stature. He went missing after crashing into the sea on 3rd August 1941 near Boulogne, and was never seen again.

◆ Group Captain Douglas Bader swings one of his "tin" legs into the cockpit of a Spitfire that bears his personal code letters "DB". Bader was about to lead the Thanksgiving Flypast over London on 15th September 1945, the fifth anniversary of the Battle of Britain. Note that the crowbar, usually stowed on the hinged cockpit door, appears to be missing.

Daily Mirror

No. 11,443
Registered at the G.P.O. as a Newspaper
ONE PENNY

DAILY MIRROR, Monday, August 19, 1940

140-16: R.A.F.'s BIGGEST VICTORY

THE GERMAN AIR FORCE, RENEWING MASS RAIDS ON SOUTH AND SOUTH-EAST ENGLAND YESTERDAY AFTER SATURDAY'S LULL, LOST AT LEAST 140 MACHINES. ONLY SIXTEEN R.A.F. FIGHTERS WERE LOST; EIGHT PILOTS WERE SAFE.

U.S., CANADA FIX JOINT DEFENCE

U.S. WARNED BY GERMANY

RAF FIRE FRENCH HARBOUR

NO RIGHT TO REFUSE SHELTER

MOTORISTS CAN AID AFTER RAIDS

"TORPEDOED" SOS

Daily Mirror

ONE PENNY

Registered at the G.P.O. as a Newspaper

MON., Monday, July 29, 1940

NEW NAZI AIR TRICK FAILS

GERMANY has been driven to employ new tactics in coastal raids on Britain — her Messerschmitt 109 single-seater fighters are now being used as dive-bombers.

9 BRITONS SEIZED BY JAPANESE

ABDICATION K.C. FLIES TO SEE THE DUKE

R.A.F. RAID ON THREE ITALIAN TOWNS REPORT

PEER QUITS HIS JOB AT THE M.O.I.

R.A.F. NEW AIR CHIEF

HER AT 4

The Most Successful Spitfire

Records from the Second World War have shown that Spitfire Mark IX, EN398, was the most successful Spitfire in action. Built in 1943 at the Supermarine Shadow Factory at Chattis Hill, it made its maiden flight on 13th February 1943 and was delivered to RAF Kenley, Surrey, where it was allocated to No. 402 Squadron, RCAF.

On 16th March 1943, Acting Wing Commander J E "Johnnie" Johnson took command of the four Canadian squadrons based at Kenley. On a tour of his new unit, Johnson came across a brand-new Mark IX Spitfire, EN398, a mark he had yet to fly. After a familiarization test flight, he claimed it as his personal mount and replaced the aircraft's squadron code letters (AE- *) with his initials, JE-J. He also had the Spitfire's guns reharmonized such that their rounds converged at a single focal point ahead of the aircraft, rather than a circular pattern several yards in diameter. His logic was difficult to contradict; instead of hitting the target with just a few rounds, an accurate attack would bring the full weight of the Spitfire's armament to bear on an enemy aircraft.

Just a couple of weeks later, Johnson and EN398 scored their first victory together, shooting down a Focke-Wulf 190 fighter. In the next five months, Johnson and "JE-J" had shot down 12 enemy aircraft, "shared" five others, damaged six with another "shared" damaged. Ultimately, the scrap merchant succeeded where the Luftwaffe failed – in October 1949, the most successful fighter aircraft of the war met her end.

◀ Mark XIV Spitfire fighters on patrol in England during the Second World War, September 1944. The aircraft bear the code letters "DW" denoting they are from No. 610 (County of Chester) Squadron.

▶ Pictured in the cockpit of his favourite Spitfire Mark IX, EN398, is Johnnie Johnson at RAF Kenley while serving with 144 Wing in 1943.

Sergeant S W Loader of New Barnet climbs into his Spitfire fighter plane to join a sweep over the English Channel in February 1944.

The wartime caption of this photo says, "A group of RAF Spitfire pilots who took part in a raid over Germany looking at their map after returning to base. The pilots, flying alone into Germany for the first time, flew over territory between Aix La Chappele and Cologne shooting up Nazi fighters, railway wagons and locomotives before returning to base without loss. April 1944."

"The 'Spitfire' is a single-seat day and night fighter monoplane in which much of the pioneer work done by the Supermarine Company in the design and construction of high-speed seaplanes for the Schneider Trophy Contests has been incorporated. The latest technique developed by the Company in flush-rivetted stressed-skin construction has been used, giving exceptional cleanliness and stiffness to wings and fuselage for a structure weight never before attained in this class of aircraft. The 'Spitfire' is fitted with a Rolls-Royce 'Merlin' engine, retractable undercarriage and split trailing-edge flaps. It is claimed to be the fastest military aeroplane in the world."

– Supermarine's publicity of their new fighter in 1936

◗ The cockpit of a restored Spitfire Mark V.

The Spitfire – Facts and Figures

There are around 50 Spitfires and a handful of Seafires currently in flying condition around the world: this number is unlikely to increase significantly with the passage of time. Other examples exist as static exhibits in museums and private collections. Many have been lovingly restored, some from remains that would, to the casual observer, otherwise be considered to be merely pieces of scrap metal. A small group of dedicated, specialist engineering companies engage in the manufacture of replacement parts, in order to keep the relatively small number of this iconic aircraft in the air. Without their efforts, the sight and sound of the Spitfire in its rightful element, the air, could not be experienced by those of a generation brought up in the jet age. Each time a Spitfire flies, it does so in tribute to the skill of its designer, the men and women who built and maintained it, and those who flew this elegant but deadly machine. The following section gives some of the background facts and figures surrounding one of Britain's most famous creations, the legendary Spitfire.

▶ A fine study of Spitfire VC, AR501, on display at Old Warden in September 1991. Belonging to the Shuttleworth Trust, AR501 was built by Westland Aircraft at Yeovil and issued to No. 310 (Czech) Squadron at Duxford in 1942. It is the only remaining Spitfire still flying with an original de Havilland three-bladed propeller.

MARK V:

Crew:	One
Length:	29ft 11in (9.12m)
Wingspan:	36ft 10in (11.23m)
Height:	11ft 5in (3.86m)
Wing area:	242.1ft² (22.48m²)
Aerofoil:	NACA 2209.4(tip)
Weights	
Empty:	5,090lb (2,309kg)
Normal loaded:	6,622lb (3,000kg)
Maximum take-off:	6,770lb (3,071kg)
Power plant	
Type:	1 × Rolls-Royce Merlin 45-series
Power output:	1,470hp (1,096kW) at 9,250ft (2,820m)
Performance	
Maximum speed:	378mph (330kn, 605km/h) at 13,000ft (3,960m)
Combat radius:	410nm (470 miles, 760km)
Ferry range:	991nm (1,140 miles, 1,840km)
Service ceiling:	35,000ft (11,300m)
Rate of climb:	3,240ft/min (16.5m/s)
Wing loading:	27.35lb/ft² (133.5kg/m²)
Power/mass ratio:	0.22hp/lb (0.36kW/kg)
Armament	
Guns:	Four 20mm Hispano Mark II cannon and four 0.303in Browning machine-guns

MARK XIV:

Crew:	One
Length:	30ft 0in (9.14m)
Wingspan:	36ft 10in (11.23m)
Height:	10ft 0in (3.05m)
Wing area:	242.1ft² (22.48m²)
Aerofoil:	NACA 2209.4 (tip)
Weights	
Empty:	6,578lb (2,984kg)
Normal loaded:	7,923lb (3,593kg)
Maximum take-off:	8,488lb (3,850kg)
Power plant	
Type:	1 × Rolls-Royce Griffon 65-series
Power output:	2,050hp (1,528kW) at 8,000ft (2,438m)
Performance	
Maximum speed:	447mph (391kn, 717km/h) at 25,600ft (7,803m)
Combat radius:	400nm (459 miles, 740km)
Ferry range:	950nm (1,090 miles, 1,815km)
Service ceiling:	43,500ft (13,258m)
Rate of climb:	3,650ft/min (18.5m/s)
Wing loading:	32.72lb/ft² (159.8kg/m²)
Power/mass ratio:	0.24hp/lb (0.42kW/kg)
Armament	
Guns:	Two 20mm (0.787in) Hispano Mark II cannon, 120rpg and four 0.303in (7.7mm) Browning machine-guns, 350rpg – replaced by two 0.50in (12.7mm) M2 Browning machine-guns, 250rpg in Mark XIVE
Bombs:	Two × 250lb (113kg) bombs

▶ Spitfire IXE, MJ730, pictured at Cranfield on 7th July 1996. The CO of No. 32 Squadron, Sqn Ldr George Silvester DFC, picked MJ730 as his personal aircraft. Being asked about his preferred choice of individual letter, he jokingly remarked that because he was squadron commander he belonged to neither "A" nor "B" Flight. By the following morning, the ground crew had painted a large "?" in place of the individual code letter. Silvester was amused by this, and so it remained; MJ730 became known as "The CO's Query".

Wing Types and Armament

Most Spitfires were built with one of the four different wing types, A, B, C and D, all of which had similar dimensions and plan, but different internal arrangements of armament and fuel tanks.

A-wing: The original wing design, its armament was eight 0.303-calibre Browning machine-guns with 300 rounds per gun (rpg), and four guns per wing.

B-wing: Based on the A-wing, it was modified to carry a 20mm Hispano cannon with 60rpg in place of the inner machine-gun.

C-wing: Also known as the "Universal wing", was structurally modified to simplify manufacture, while allowing mixed types of armament, as for the A- and B-wings, or a new combination of four, short-barrelled 20mm Hispano cannon with 120rpg. Hard points for a 250lb bomb were provided outboard of each wheel well. The visual undercarriage position pins of earlier marks were deleted from the Mark IX and later marks.

D-wing: This designation was the unarmed, long-range wing for reconnaissance versions. Additional fuel capacity was provided within the leading edge ahead of the wing spar, each tank capable of carrying 66 gallons.

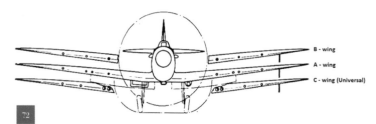

B - wing
A - wing
C - wing (Universal)

◀ Spitfire wing types and armament layout – frontal views.

A modern Tornado in stark contrast to its Second World War predecessor, the Spitfire, which features the original A-wing armament with eight machine-guns.

This Spitfire IX is in the colours of No. 316 (Polish) Squadron of the RAF and represents the aircraft flown by Flt Lt Lew Kurylowicz DFC.

E-wing: Introduced in early 1944, this was structurally unchanged from the C-wing. The outer machine-gun ports were deleted; each inner gun bay could accommodate either one of the two weapon fits: (1) a 20mm Hispano Mark II cannon with 120rpg in the outer position and an American 0.50 calibre M2 Browning machine-gun with 250rpg inboard; or (2) two 20mm Hispano cannon with 120rpg.

Clipped wings: Starting with the Mark V, some Spitfires had their classic, elliptical wing tips replaced by shorter, squared-off fairings to enhance their rate of roll. Clipped-wing Spitfires are sometimes erroneously referred to as "LF" versions, e.g. LF Mark VB. The "LF" designation rightfully refers to those Spitfires fitted with the low-altitude version of the Rolls-Royce Merlin engine: not all LF Spitfires had the clipped wings.

Extended wing-tips: From the Mark VI, pointed wing-tips were fitted to high-altitude versions of the Spitfire, their larger area giving improvements in climb rate and maximum service ceiling. Manoeuvrability was, however, compromised in combat situations at normal altitudes. From the Mark XIII, tips were interchangeable, giving greater flexibility in operational situations.

The entirely revised (or "new wing"): Beginning with the Mark 21, the Spitfire had a totally new, restructured wing design. An enlarged plan form, with a wider chord towards the tips, accommodated larger ailerons; the tips were squared-off, thus losing the elliptical outline that was the Spitfire's signature feature. Four even shorter-barrelled, Hispano Mark II or V cannon confirmed the RAF's all-cannon armament policy. Now fully enclosed when retracted, a longer and wider-track undercarriage increased the ground clearance, allowing a larger diameter propeller to be fitted. No official designation was ever given to this wing type, it being most often referred to as the "new wing".

◀ A Browning 0.50in heavy machine-gun round (left), in comparison with a 0.303in round.

A PR Mark XI, with the clean leading edges denoting its D-wing, pictured over the south of England on the 60th Anniversary of the Battle of Britain, September 2000.

MH434, a Mark IXB, is one of the most active Spitfires on the air display scene and has starred in several Spitfire-related films, including *The Battle of Britain* television series and videos. Built in 1943, this aircraft is owned and operated by The Old Flying Machine Company, Duxford.

Operators of the Spitfire

Spitfires were purchased and flown by many nations. The following national governments and air forces flew various marks of the type, either during or after the Second World War:

Argentina (two ex-civilian, test only)	Hong Kong	Rhodesia
Australia	India (Union of India)	South Africa
Belgium	Indonesia	Soviet Union
British Raj (Indian Sub-continent)	Ireland	Sweden
Burma	Israel	Syria
Canada	Italy (Kingdom and Republic)	Thailand
Czechoslovakia	Netherlands	Turkey
Denmark	New Zealand	United Kingdom
Egypt	Norway	United States of America
France	Pakistan	Yugoslavia
Free France	Poland	
Greece	Portugal	

◗ The Spitfire was used by many foreign air forces. This Mark VB, BM635, bears the code letters of the US 309th Fighter Squadron.

"It was a super aircraft, it was absolutely. It was so sensitive on the controls. There was no heaving, or pulling and pushing and kicking. You just breathed on it and when you wanted, if you wanted to turn, you just moved your hands slowly and she went... She really was the perfect flying machine. I've never flown anything sweeter. I've flown jets right up to the Venom, but nothing, nothing like her. Nothing like a Spitfire."

— George Unwin, No. 19 Squadron RAF during the Battle of Britain

◗ A line-up of 12 Spitfires awaiting their camera call in the film *The Battle of Britain*, North Weald, May 1968.

The Spitfire – Top Twenty Facts

Fact 1 – Early Spitfire pilots were more familiar with fixed undercarriage aircraft. Because of this, many accidents were due to pilots forgetting to lower the Spitfire's retractable landing gear.

Fact 2 – The Spitfire was the only British aircraft to remain in continuous production throughout the Second World War.

Fact 3 – Most of the aerial combat scenes in the 1969 film *The Battle of Britain* were filmed using Spitfires, due to the small number of Hurricanes remaining in flying condition at the time. This factor probably led to the Hurricane, which was more numerous at the time of the actual battle, receiving less credit than it deserved.

Fact 4 – Fighter-bomber versions of the Spitfire could carry one 250- or 500lb (115- or 230kg) bomb, beneath the fuselage, and a 250lb bomb under each wing.

Fact 5 – On Battle of Britain Day, 15th September 1940, Spitfire pilot Sergeant Raymond Holmes spotted a German bomber heading for Central London. With no ammunition remaining, Holmes heroically decided to ram the bomber, disabling it over Victoria railway station.

◆ The Spitfire F24 featured the four cannon armament, a five-bladed propeller driven by a Rolls-Royce Griffon engine, and a full undercarriage door system, as seen here.

Fact 6 – Camouflaged Spitfires used in the film *The Battle of Britain* did not film well against land backgrounds: aerial scenes were, therefore, filmed mostly against a background of sky.

Fact 7 – After the victory in the Battle of Britain, the first patrols over France (since that country fell in December 1940), took place. These patrols were carried out by pairs of Spitfires and were known as "Rhubarbs".

Fact 8 – The Spitfire's maiden flight was on 5th March 1936. It entered service with the RAF in 1938 and remained operational until 1955. During this time, 20,351 Spitfires were built.

Fact 9 – The first public appearance of the Spitfire took place at the RAF Hendon air display on Saturday 27th June 1936.

Fact 10 – The largest Spitfire production site was at Castle Bromwich in the West Midlands, where 12,129 of the aircraft were built. At the peak of production, 320 completed Spitfires left the factory in one month.

◀ A Spitfire IX, loaded with three bombs, ready to take off from Longues-sur-Mer, Normandy, August 1944. In the cockpit is Wg Cdr A G Page DSO, OBE, DFC and Bar, whose initials "AGP" are painted below the nose. Shot down in August 1940 while flying a Hurricane during the Battle of Britain, Page was badly burned when his fuel tank was hit and caught fire. One month after this picture was taken, Page crash-landed, breaking a bone in his back. Finally grounded from operations, he had amassed a personal tally of 10 solo kills, five shared kills and three enemy aircraft damaged.

Fact 11 – Newly built Spitfires were flown by civilian pilots of the Air Transport Auxiliary, one in five of whom were women, on delivery from the factory to RAF units.

Fact 12 – It is a common myth that, when Hitler was growing frustrated with the Luftwaffe's failures in the Battle of Britain, he asked Hermann Goering: "What do you want to wipe out this air force?" and was told: "A squadron of Spitfires." According to the book, *The First and Last*, by the Luftwaffe fighter ace, General Adolf Galland, it was actually Goering, the Luftwaffe commander, who asked Galland what equipment he would like; in response, he replied, "I should like an outfit of Spitfires for my group."

Fact 13 – One of the names suggested for the Spitfire during production was the "Shrew".

Fact 14 – In late 1943, Spitfires powered by Rolls-Royce Griffon engines, developing as much as 2,050hp, began entering service. Capable of top speeds of 440mph (710km/h) and a ceiling of 40,000ft (12,200m), these were particularly effective against V-1 flying bombs.

Fact 15 – Fighter versions of the Spitfire were gradually withdrawn from RAF service during the early 1950s, but photo-reconnaissance Spitfires continued in mainstream RAF service until 1954. By 1957, the only three remaining airworthy Spitfires were being flown by civilian pilots of the Temperature and Humidity Monitoring (THUM) Flight at RAF Woodvale. With their operational careers over, these three Spitfire PR XIXs (PM631, PS853 and PS915) were flown to RAF Biggin Hill on 11th July 1957, to form the nucleus of the Historic Aircraft Flight (HAF), the precursor to the Battle of Britain Memorial Flight (BBMF).

◆ On opposing sides in the Second World War, a Messerschmitt Bf 109 "Black 6" and a late model Griffon-engined low-back Spitfire, fly peaceably together over southern England, c. 1996.

Fact 16 – Built in larger numbers than any other Spitfire variant, deliveries to the RAF of the Mark V commenced in 1941. Flown by famous pilots such as Ian Gleed, Al Deere, Don Kingaby and Johnnie Johnson, the classic Mark V remained in service until the end of the war.

Fact 17 – Over 1,300 Spitfires were loaned to Russia in a lend-lease scheme in the spring of 1943. The initial batch of fighters included around 150 Mark VBs, many of which had seen some hard service with the RAF. Soviet pilots were not particularly enamoured with the Spitfire, due to its unfavourable ground-handling characteristics on the rough landing strips from which they operated. The narrow track of the undercarriage, coupled with a tendency to "nose-over" under braking, caused many incidents.

Fact 18 – Sqn Ldr Donald O Finlay, OC 41 Squadron, flying his brand new, personal Spitfire IIA, P7666, EB-Z, claimed a destroyed Me 109 on his first sortie on the day the aircraft was delivered, 23rd November 1940.

Fact 19 – During the land offensive in Europe, some Spitfires underwent Modification XXX, which enabled them to carry a beer barrel instead of a bomb under each wing: the barrels and their precious contents were landed (not dropped!) and provided a morale-boosting taste of home for British and Allied personnel.

Fact 20 – When production ceased in 1947, 20,334 Spitfires of all versions had been produced, 2,053 of them were Griffon-powered versions.

⬧ Catching the sunlight at an air show in 1995, the elegant lines of a Spitfire XIX are displayed to the crowd below.

Code Names for Fighter Operations

"Ramrods" – Otherwise called "fighter sweeps" – were large-scale attacks by huge formations of fighters over enemy territory. They were often carried out at the same time as bomber raids, in an attempt to divert German fighters away from Allied bomber formations.

"Rhubarbs" – These were smaller-scale attacks on targets of opportunity in enemy-held territory, usually carried out by a small number of fighters or ground-attack aircraft.

"Rodeos" – Were seek-and-destroy raids by small numbers of fighters.

"Rhubarbs" and "Rodeos" were usually carried out at very low level, often at tree-top height, to minimize detection by German radar and direction-finding equipment. Attacks were carried out on enemy airfields, military installations, factories, roads, railways and canal transport.

"Circuses" – The above-mentioned types of attack were collectively known as "circuses". By late 1943, these attacks were concentrated around Calais in northern France, an area well within the reach of Spitfires from the Hornchurch Wing. Apart from the damage they caused, these attacks were also intended as diversionary raids to deceive the enemy into believing a forthcoming invasion would take place in that vicinity, rather than on the beaches of Normandy, which eventually took place in 1944.

◆ MH434, a Spitfire IX, being put through its paces at the former Battle of Britain airfield at Biggin Hill, May 1980.

Presentation and Donated Spitfires

▶ An unnamed Spitfire pilot of No. 603 (City of Edinburgh) Squadron inspects the mascot painted on the side of his Spitfire. On 16th October 1939 this squadron destroyed the first enemy aircraft to be shot down over Britain in the Second World War.

Patriotic individuals, as well as towns, countries of the Commonwealth and other organizations, were encouraged to donate the cost of a Spitfire. The nominal cost of a Spitfire was set by the government at £5,000, a substantial sum at the time, although the real cost of manufacturing each aircraft was more than £10,000. In recognition, the donor was permitted to christen their individual Spitfire with a name of their choosing.

Approximately 1,500 of the donated or "presentation" Spitfires, representing about 17 per cent of total production, were funded by public or individual subscription. One such Spitfire was flown by Barrie Heath and saw active service in 1940 with No. 611 Squadron, RAF. His aircraft was a Spitfire IIA, P7883, named "Grahame Heath", which had been donated by his parents in memory of his brother, a pilot in the Royal Flying Corps, who had been killed in the First World War. Barrie Heath was an outspoken character; when criticized by his squadron commander, Sqn Ldr James McComb, for damaging his Spitfire on landing, Heath is said to have replied, somewhat arrogantly: "This is my Spit and I'll fly it any b****y way I like."

◀ Barrie Heath is seen here standing on his Spitfire which had been donated by his parents and named in memory of his brother, Grahame Heath, who was shot down and killed in the First World War.

Speed and Altitude Records

Beginning in late 1943, high-speed diving trials were undertaken at Farnborough to investigate the handling characteristics of an aircraft travelling at speeds close to the speed of sound, i.e. the onset of aerodynamic compressibility effects. Because it had the highest limiting Mach number of any aircraft at that time, a Spitfire XI was chosen to take part in these trials. It was during these trials that EN409, flown by Sqn Ldr J R Tobin, reached 606mph (975km/h, Mach 0.891) in a 45-degree dive. In April 1944, in another dive, while being flown by Sqn Ldr Anthony F Martindale, the same aircraft suffered a catastrophic engine failure when the propeller and reduction gear broke off. He successfully glided the Spitfire 20 miles (32km) back to the airfield and landed safely. Martindale was awarded the Air Force Cross for his exceptional skill and courage.

On 5th February 1952, a Spitfire Mark XIX of No. 81 Squadron, based at Kai Tak in Hong Kong, reached probably the highest altitude ever achieved by a Spitfire. Its pilot, Flt Lt Ted Powles, was on a routine flight to report on meteorological conditions at various altitudes. He climbed to an indicated altitude of 50,000ft (15,240m), a true altitude of 51,550ft (15,712m).

◀ Spitfire XI, EN 409, was used in high-speed diving trials in 1944. Note the damage to the engine where the reduction gear and propeller broke off and also damage to the wing leading edge.

Spitfire PS893, a Mark XIX of the Battle of Britain Memorial Flight, pictured in September 1966.

We will remember them